HOW DO WE KNOW
The Bible
Is True?

HOW DO WE KNOW
The Bible
Is True?

Reasons a kid can believe it.

Lynn Waller

ZondervanPublishingHouse

Grand Rapids, Michigan

A Division of HarperCollinsPublishers

How Do We Know the Bible Is True?
Copyright © 1991 by Lynn Waller

Requests for information should be addressed to:
Zondervan Publishing House
Grand Rapids, Michigan 49530

Library of Congress Cataloging-in-Publication Data

Waller, Lynn.
    How do we know the Bible is true? : reasons a kid can believe it /
Lynn Waller.
        p. cm.
    Summary: presents reasons why the people, places, and events of
the Bible were real people, places, and events.
    ISBN 0-310-53821-1 (pbk.)
    1. Bible—Evidences, authority, etc.—Juvenile literature.
[1. Bible] I. Title.
BS480.W235 1991
220.1—dc20   91–25296
                                                                  CIP
                                                                   AC

Edited by Dave Lambert
Designed and illustrated by Tim Davis

Printed in the United States of America

97 / CH / 10 9 8 7 6 5

To my daughter, Wendy,
who gave me the idea for this book.

and

To my son, Landon,
who encouraged me to finish it.

Contents

HOW DO WE KNOW THE BIBLE IS TRUE?

Science in the Bible

WHERE DID HAND WASHING COME FROM?

In our modern world, almost everyone knows that it's important to keep clean. But people haven't always known that. In fact, it was just a little over one hundred years ago that we discovered it.

In the 1840s a doctor in Austria named Ignaz Semmelweis was concerned about the women in his hospital. Too many of the mothers who were there to have a baby were dying. He wanted to find out why.

Dr. Semmelweis noticed that many of the women were being treated by doctors who had just finished doing autopsies. (An autopsy is an operation on a

dead person to find out why he died.) After the autopsies, the doctors would examine the live patients without washing their hands first. So Dr. Semmelweis decided to try a new rule: All doctors and nurses had to wash their hands after handling the dead bodies before they could touch the live patients.

Guess what happened? The number of deaths went down immediately.

Later, Dr. Semmelweis tried his discovery at another hospital. It worked beautifully there too.

Within the next thirty years, scientific discoveries about germs proved that Dr. Semmelweis was right, and why. But really, Dr. Semmelweis wasn't the first to know that cleanliness is healthy. It had been in the Bible for more than 3,000 years!

God told Moses in the book of Numbers, chapter 19, to wash after touching a dead body. Also, in Leviticus 13 and 14, God told the Israelites how to keep open sores and other skin diseases from spreading.

It took man thousands of years to find out why those things were in the Bible.

WHAT HOLDS UP THE EARTH?

That question has puzzled mankind for thousands of years. In India, they thought the earth was resting on the backs of several large elephants. The elephants were resting on the back of a very large turtle. The turtle was either resting on a snake or swimming in a sea of milk.

Others said the earth was on the back of a catfish swimming in an ocean. According to the Greeks, a god named Atlas had the difficult job of holding the earth on his shoulders.

But the Bible says that God "hangs the earth on nothing" (Job 26:7, ICB). And today we know that that is true: The earth is suspended in space. It isn't sitting on anything!

But when the book of Job was written, people didn't know that. How did the writers of the Bible know it? Only God could have revealed it to them.

4

Another thing people believed in biblical times (and for hundreds of years afterward) was that the earth was flat. If you went too far, you would fall off the edge!

Now, of course, we know that the earth is round. In the 1500s Ferdinand Magellan's men were the first to sail all the way around the world. That helped prove the roundness of the earth.

But that too was revealed in Scripture long before man discovered it. For example, Isaiah 40:22, (ICB) says, "God sits on his throne above the circle of the earth."

The roundness of the earth is shown in another way in Luke 17. There Jesus tells about his Second Coming. He said, "On that night two people will be in one bed; one will be taken and the other left" (NIV). But even though some people will be in bed when Christ comes again, the next verse tells us that it will also be *daytime* when he comes, because people will be grinding grain—something that was always done during daylight.

How can it be daylight and dark at the same time? If the earth is flat, it *can't.* But the earth is round, and that means it's always daytime on one side and night on the other. They didn't know that in Jesus' time. But he did. And there it is in the Bible.

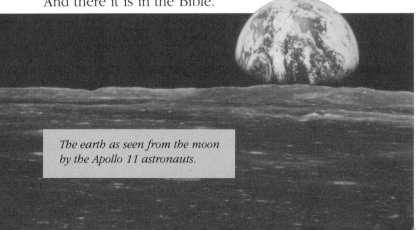

The earth as seen from the moon by the Apollo 11 astronauts.

Ancient people were often afraid of the sun, moon, and stars. This was because they thought these things were alive. The Egyptians believed that stars were the souls of dead people who had become gods. Others thought that since the stars looked smaller than the moon, they must be the moon's children.

But the Bible's first chapter (Genesis 1) points out that the sun, moon, and stars were created by God. This lets us know that they are not living beings to be feared.

Eclipses are a good example. An eclipse happens when the sun's light is blocked by the earth or moon for a short time. Usually, the moon is bright

because it reflects the sun's light. But when the earth blocks that light, the moon looks like it's disappearing. Also, when the moon comes between the earth and the sun, it looks to us like the sun is disappearing.

Above: A complete solar eclipse.
Right: The sun's corona as seen during an eclipse.

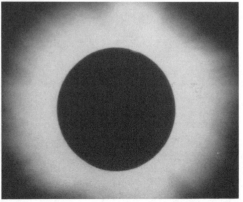

HICCUP

This was very frightening to people long ago. The Chaldeans, who lived close to the Israelites, thought that eclipses happened when the moon was mad at the earth and turned its face away. The Chinese believed that an eclipse was caused by a demon or some huge animal that ate the sun. That *would* be scary, wouldn't it?

But God told Jeremiah, "Don't be afraid of special signs in the sky, even though the other nations are afraid of them" (Jer. 10:2, ICB). God went on to reassure Jeremiah that the universe is under God's control (Jer. 10:12-13).

People who didn't know the Scriptures continued to be afraid of the skies for hundreds of years. Later, scientists learned that the heavenly bodies were not alive and that we should not fear them. Of course, that's what the Bible told us all along.

WHAT'S IN THE OCEAN?

Until modern times, no one knew what the bottom of the ocean was like. People thought it was like the deserts, flat and sandy. They believed the ocean floor was mostly saucer shaped, and deepest in the middle.

But in the 1900s, oceanographers found that the sea has many deep valleys or canyons. The deepest of these canyons are called trenches. Some are amazingly deep.

continent   continental shelf   continental slope   island

trench

For example, the Marianas trench in the Pacific is so deep that if you dropped Mt. Everest (29,000 feet high) into it, the peak would still be a mile below the surface.

Just as there are valleys in the ocean, so there are underwater mountains. In the Atlantic Ocean, there is a range of undersea mountains 10,000 miles long. A few of these rise above the surface and form islands.

But 3,000 years ago, the Bible mentioned both the valleys and the mountains of the sea. David wrote a psalm praising God for rescuing him from his enemies. He spoke of God being the maker of "the valleys of the sea" (2 Sam. 22:16 and Psalm 18:15, NIV). One of the questions God asks Job is, "Have you walked in the valleys of the sea?"(Job 38:16, ICB). The prophet Jonah talked about "mountains in the sea" (Jonah 2:6, ICB).

These parts of the Bible are not talking about oceanography. They are discussing man's relation to God. Even so, how did the writers of the Bible know about the mountains and valleys of the ocean thousands of years before scientists discovered them?

Somebody told them. And I have an idea who it was!

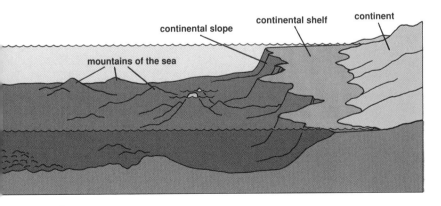

continental slope   continental shelf   continent

mountains of the sea

atthew Maury was an officer in the U. S. Navy. He had always been interested in the oceans and also enjoyed reading the Bible. One day he was reading from Psalm 8 about how God has put man over the animals, birds, fish, and all the creatures that swim in "the paths of the seas" (8:8, NIV).

That last part grabbed his attention. He thought, *I didn't know there were paths in the sea.* But he was sure that, if the Bible said there were paths in the sea, then there must be such things. So he set out to discover them. And he did.

Maury discovered that the world's oceans have many paths, or currents, which are like rivers flowing through the sea. He wrote the first textbook on oceanographic physics and became known as "the pathfinder of the seas" and "the father of modern navigation." His discovery and his books helped make ocean travel easier and quicker.

Isn't it interesting that Matthew Maury got his idea about the ocean currents from reading a poem written more than 2,000 years earlier by a man who probably never saw an ocean? That should give us another clue about who is really behind the writing of the Bible.

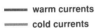

━━━ warm currents
━━━ cold currents

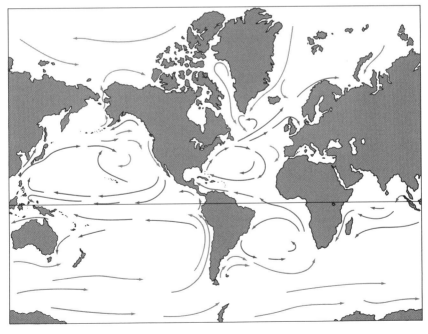

For thousands of years, doctors often treated sick people by a practice called "bleeding." They would cut a vein and drain blood from the patient. Why? Because people thought that diseases started in the blood. So, if you got rid of some blood, it would help you get well.

In December of 1799, George Washington became very ill. His doctors bled him four times in one day. In a few hours, he was dead.

In some parts of the world, folk healers still bleed their patients. But most doctors now know that bleeding doesn't help a sick person. It does just the opposite. That's because the blood carries to every part of our body the things we need to stay alive. Removing blood makes it harder for the blood that's left in the body to do its job.

And that's what the Bible said in Leviticus 17:11 (ICB): "The life of the body is in the blood." Isn't it sad that, in George Washington's time, they didn't realize how true that verse is?

What the Bible tells us about blood is evidence that it is the Word of God, since no one else knew that at the time the Bible was written. But what the Bible *doesn't* say can also tell us that it came from God. And here's an example.

12

The Egyptians of Moses' time knew more about medicine than any other people. Yet they had some strange treatments. If a person had a deep splinter that got infected, they would put worm's blood or donkey manure on the sore spot. When children were sick, doctors often gave them skinned baby mice to eat. The list of such remedies is long.

Remember that Moses wrote Leviticus and most of the first five books of the Bible. He was raised as the King of Egypt's son. And "the Egyptians taught Moses all the things they knew" (Acts 7:22, ICB). Yet not one of these weird treatments is mentioned in the Bible.

Other ancient books are filled with such harmful medical advice. How did Moses and the other writers of the Bible know to leave all of that out?

COME IN OUT OF THE RAIN

Lightning, thunder, and rainstorms have bothered man for thousands of years. In Bible times, people from Rome to Egypt to India thought lightning bolts were missiles thrown by the gods. The Chinese even thought lightning was a goddess. Her job was to flash light here and there to help the thunder god find the people he was mad at.

Since rain is so necessary to our life on earth, ancient people wondered what caused it. Some thought sprinkling water on the ground would help cause rain. Others tried to stab holes in the clouds with spears. Maybe the most unusual idea is found in one of the *Vedas* (holy books of the Hindu religion in India). It says to tie up a frog with its mouth propped open. If you tie him to the right tree and say the right words, rain will fall!

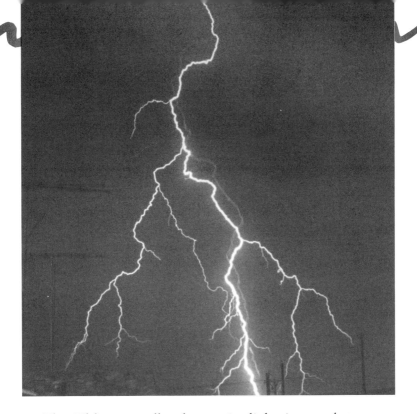

The Bible, too, talks about rain, lightning, and storms. But it includes none of the superstitious, fantastic ideas found in the other books written in those days. Instead of teaching that these forces of nature were living beings who often did crazy things, as many people believed, the Scriptures taught that the earth's weather follows rules and cycles. Notice Genesis 8:22 (ICB):

> As long as the earth continues, there will be planting and harvest. Cold and hot, summer and winter, day and night will not stop.

Job 28:26 (ICB) says, "God made rules for the rain. And he set a path for the thunderstorm to follow." God told Jeremiah, "Day and night will always come at the right time" (Jeremiah 33:20, ICB).

Many years later, scientists would begin to discover the "rules for the rain" that Job talked about. We now have weathermen who know about the path of a thunderstorm. Of course, all along the Bible had mentioned these laws of nature that we are still discovering. All along, Scripture reminded us that the laws of nature are really the laws of God.

Speaking of rain, exactly where does rain come from? Rainfall is part of a process called the water cycle. Here's how the cycle works: The sun evaporates water from the ocean. That water vapor rises and becomes clouds. This water in the clouds falls back to earth as rain, collects in streams and rivers, and makes its way back to the ocean. That process repeats itself again and again.

rain

Scientists began to discover that water follows such a cycle about 300 years ago. Galileo came up with this idea in 1630. But amazingly, the Scriptures mentioned this centuries earlier. Amos 9:6 (ICB) says that God "calls for the waters of the sea. He pours them out on the land." Long before man discovered it, the Bible told us that the water from the sea ends up falling on the land.

Another verse talks about the water cycle in a little different way. Isaiah 55:10 (ICB) shows that rain and snow return to the sky after watering the earth. "Rain and snow fall from the sky. They don't return without watering the ground."

How did Amos and Isaiah know where rain comes from? They weren't scientists. They were prophets who said they were just repeating God's message. And that must have been true, since God was the only one who knew about the water cycle 2,500 years ago.

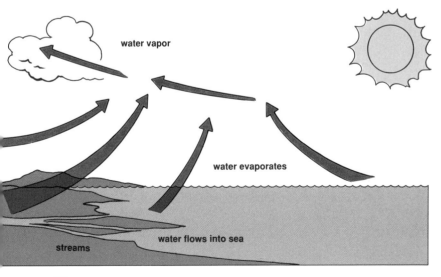

water vapor

water evaporates

water flows into sea

streams

HOW DO WE KNOW THE BIBLE IS TRUE?

Fulfilled Prophecy

ometimes, God gives a message to a person for that person to share with others. The person God gives such a message to is called a prophet. His message is called a prophecy.

Usually, a prophecy is mainly for the people of that time and place. But sometimes God enables a prophet to predict the future!

Long before Jesus was born, many prophets predicted the future by telling about him. For example, more than 700 years before Christ, the prophet Micah wrote,

> But you, Bethlehem Ephrathah, are one of the smallest towns in Judah. But from you will come one who will rule Israel for me.
>
> Micah 5:2 (ICB)

Many years later, some wise men came to Jerusalem looking for the baby Jesus. Herod asked the teachers of the Law where Christ would be born. "They answered, 'In the town of Bethlehem in Judah. The prophet wrote about this in the Scriptures'" (Matthew 2:5, ICB). So those who were familiar with the Scriptures knew that Jesus would be born in Bethlehem. They just didn't know when.

Modern Bethlehem, with the Church of the Nativity at top center.

But when the wise men saw his star, they knew the time had come. So they went to Bethlehem as the Scripture had said, and of course, he was there.

Another prophecy that came true is the one made by David in Psalm 16:10 (ICB). David lived about 1,000 years before Christ. He wrote,

> You will not leave me in the grave.
> You will not let your Holy One rot.

But David wasn't talking about himself. As Peter said in Acts 2:31 (ICB), "David was talking about the Christ rising from death." Peter was a witness to Jesus rising from death. But David had predicted it 1,000 years before.

ouldn't it be amazing if someone could tell fifteen facts about a person—and do it 800 years before the person was born? Well, that's what the Old Testament prophet Isaiah did. His description of Jesus was so detailed it could have fit no one else. Notice how well Jesus fits all fifteen of Isaiah's predictions in the chart below.

ISAIAH'S VISION

DESCRIPTION	PREDICTED	FULFILLED
(1) hated	(Isaiah 53:3)	Matt. 27:39–43
(2) a man of sadness	(53:3)	Matt. 26:38
(3) familiar with suffering	(53:3)	Heb. 4:15
(4) rejected by his people	(53:3)	John 1:10–11
(5) taking our suffering for us	(53:4)	Matt. 8:16–17
(6) without sin	(53:9)	1 Pet. 2:22
(7) silent to his accusers	(53:7)	Matt. 26:63; 27:12

Early Christians used Isaiah's prophecy as a starting place to tell people who Jesus was and what he did. For example, in Acts chapter 8 a man from the African country of Ethiopia was reading Isaiah 53. He was curious about who Isaiah was describing. When the man asked Philip that question, Philip "started with this same Scripture and told the man the Good News about Jesus" (Acts 8:35, ICB). And that Scripture about Jesus was written 800 years before his birth.

DESCRIPTION	PREDICTED	FULFILLED
(8) taking our sins on himself	(53:5)	1 Cor. 15:3
(9) taking our punishment	(53:5)	1 Pet. 2:24–25
(10) treated like a criminal	(53:12)	Luke 22:37
(11) asking for our forgiveness	(53:12)	Luke 23:34
(12) treated unjustly	(53:8)	Matt. 27:24
(13) buried with rich people	(53:9)	Matt. 27:57–60
(14) raised from death	(53:10)	Luke 24:6–8
(15) honored	(53:12)	Phil. 2:9–11

Tyre was a powerful and wealthy city. Part of the city was on the coast, but some of the people lived on an island a half mile out in the ocean. The people of Tyre were famous for making purple dye and beautiful glassware. But they were also very evil.

About 586 B.C., the prophet Ezekiel reported what God had told him about Tyre. First, he said, Tyre would be attacked by Nebuchadnezzar's Babylonian army and later by other nations. Next, the city would be destroyed so completely that its wood and rock would be scraped up and thrown into the sea. It would not be rebuilt; it would be just a place for fishermen to spread their nets.

Shortly after this prophecy, Nebuchadnezzar did surround and attack the mainland part of the city. The battle went on for thirteen years. Finally, the Babylonians broke down the walls and tore up the city. But many of the people of Tyre escaped in boats to the island. So Nebuchadnezzar, even though he conquered the city, didn't fulfill Ezekiel's prophecy.

But 250 years later, Alexander the Great and his Greek army wanted to capture the island city. How

could a marching army get to it? There was a half-mile of water between them and the island. Then someone had an idea: Why not take the ruins of the mainland city and dump them in the ocean? This would make a walkway out to the island. So they scraped up all the wood, rock, and dust from the old city and built a road for the army to attack on. It worked perfectly, and the job of destroying Tyre was completed.

Later, another city called Tyre was built nearby, but not on the same location. For 2,000 years, fishermen have used the spot where old Tyre was as a place to spread their nets.

It all happened just as the prophet had said in Ezekiel 26:1-14. But how could Ezekiel have known what would happen 250 years in the future? There's only one explanation. It was just as Ezekiel said: "The Lord spoke his word to me." (26:1, ICB)

The ruins of Babylon in modern-day Iraq.

Babylon was the capital of the Chaldean empire and the mightiest city in the world. Its walls were 200 feet high and 187 feet thick. The huge brass gates and 300-foot-high towers for watchmen made it seem impossible to defeat. But while Babylon was at the height of its power, God's prophets said it would end.

Isaiah wrote, "Babylon is the most beautiful of all kingdoms. The Babylonians are very proud of it. But God will destroy it like Sodom and Gomorrah." (Isa. 13:19, ICB) Sodom and Gomorrah were two wicked cities that had been wiped out and never rebuilt.

Another prophet, Jeremiah, said this:

> This is what the Lord of heaven's armies says;
> "Babylon's thick wall will be pulled down.
> Her high gates will be burned . . .
> No people or animals will live in it. It will be an
>   empty ruin forever."

(Jer. 51:58, 62, ICB)

Long after Isaiah and Jeremiah were dead, the Persians captured Babylon. Later, Alexander the Great and his Greek army took it from the Persians.

Alexander was one of the greatest military men in history. He ruled a huge area from Greece to India. He decided to rebuild Babylon and make it his capital city. But after giving the order to rebuild it, Alexander got sick and died at the age of 33. His order was not carried out. Even the most powerful man in the world cannot do something if God says it will not happen!

Six hundred years later, a Roman ruler named Julian (who didn't believe the Bible) was leading an army to fight the Persians. Part of Babylon's walls were still standing. To keep the Persians from using those walls, he had what was left of them completely leveled. And so a man who tried to keep people from believing the Bible actually helped make its words come true.

In its days of glory, Babylon had the most beautiful gardens in the world. Those Hanging Gardens were considered one of the seven wonders of the ancient world. But today the spot where Babylon stood is a barren desert. Just as the Bible said it would be.

The Edomites were a powerful nation for hundreds of years. They were neighbors of the Israelites. In a way, they were also relatives, because the people of Edom were the descendants of Esau. The Israelites were the descendants of Esau's brother, Jacob. But the two groups were not usually on friendly terms with each other. Because the Edomites mistreated Israel and even stole from God's temple, God decided to punish them.

Several prophets told what would happen to them. Obadiah gave this message from God:

> "Your home is up high.
> And you say to yourself,
> 'No one can bring me down
>   to the ground . . .'
> But I will bring you down
>   from there," says the Lord.
> (Obadiah 3, 4, ICB)

The Edomites lived in forts built high in the rocks. They were sure no one could ever defeat them. But Isaiah said their strong cities would become deserted:

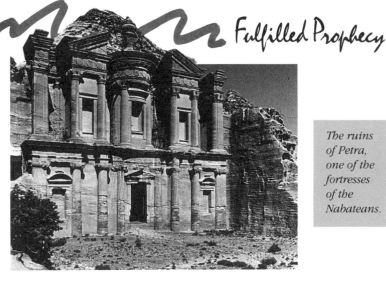

The ruins of Petra, one of the fortresses of the Nabateans.

> God will make it an empty wasteland.
> It will have nothing left in it . . .
> Thorns will take over the strong towers.
> Wild bushes will grow in the walled cities.
> Wild dogs will live there.
> Owls will live in those homes.
>
> (Isaiah 34:11, 13)

Jeremiah had a similar message:

> "Edom will be destroyed like the cities of
>   Sodom and Gomorrah
> and the towns around them," says the Lord.
> "No one will live there!
> No man will stay in Edom".   (Jeremiah 49:18)

And that is just what happened. Within the next 200 years, the Edomites were defeated by the Arabs and later by the Nabateans. Petra, the capital city of the Nabateans, contained many temples carved into solid rock. It can still be visited today. But no one lives there. Some ruins of Edomite cities have also been found. But there, too, the only living things are weeds and wild animals. And even they help show us that the Bible is true.

Moabites and Ammonites

There were several groups of people who were strong and doing well when the Bible said they were going to be punished for their sins. The Moabites and the Ammonites are good examples. Several prophets predicted the end of those nations. Ezekiel, for instance, reported that God said:

The Moabite stone, erected by Mesha, king of Moab, and dating back to about 850 B.C. It contains over thirty lines of writing in ancient Moabite.

I will give Moab, along with the Ammonites, to the people of the East. They will take over these people. Then, along with the Ammonites, Moab will not be a nation anymore . . . And they will know that I am the Lord.

(Ezekiel 25:10-11, ICB)

The Moabites and the Ammonites were defeated by the Babylonians and the Persians. (Both came from the east.) By the year 70 A.D., both Moabites and Ammonites had disappeared—just as the Scripture had said hundreds of years earlier.

Nineveh

Nineveh (like Babylon) was a powerful city surrounded by huge walls. But God's prophet Nahum said that the city would fall and a flood would help its enemies capture it (Nahum 1:8, 2:6). Zephaniah (2:13-14) added that it would be deserted and become just a place to keep flocks and herds.

Two Elamite warriors carrying bows and a quiver, a limestone relief from Nineveh, about 668-633 B.C.

Nineveh was captured by its enemies in 612 B.C. when the Tigris River flooded and burst part of the walls, letting the attacking army in. About 200 years later, the Greek army passed through the area. They reported that there was only a pile of rubble where the mighty city had been.

As you might guess, it is still deserted today. But that place is good for one thing: grazing flocks of sheep. In fact, its modern name means "Mound of Many Sheep."

These are just a few of the many predictions of the Bible coming true exactly as the Scripture had said. But this should not surprise us. Jesus himself told the apostle John, "Write the things you see, what is now and what will happen later" (Revelation 1:19, ICB).

But why are all these predictions in the Bible? One reason is that they help us have confidence in the Scripture and in the God who gave it. I like what D. James Kennedy wrote in his book *Why I Believe* (p. 26):

Predictions are also promises. I believe that God
gave us over two thousand predictions in order
that we may learn to believe his promises. God
promised that the walls of Jerusalem would be
rebuilt; that the walls of Babylon would never be
rebuilt; that the walls of Tyre would be
destroyed; that Sidon would continue—so that
we may believe his promises.

Proof from Archaeology

WHO ARE THE HITTITES?

The Old Testament mentions a group of people called the Hittites many times. Some of them lived to the north of the Israelites. Others lived with the Israelites in the land of Canaan. Genesis 23:10 explains that Abraham bought some land from Ephron the Hittite. Later Esau married a Hittite woman. Two of David's fighting men, Uriah and Ahimelech, were Hittites.

But until about one hundred years ago, no one had found any trace or mention of the Hittites anywhere—except in the Bible. People who didn't believe the Bible said, "There's no evidence that there ever was such a people as the Hittites. If they really existed, someone else would have written about them. Or archaeologists would have found remains of their work. This shows that the Bible is wrong."

But Bible believers said, "That doesn't mean the Bible is wrong. Maybe we just haven't found the evidence of the Hittites yet. If the Scripture says it, it must be true. Just wait."

Proof from Archaeology

Sure enough—in 1906 a German named Hugo Winckler was digging in the land we now call Turkey. He found the city that was the Hittite capital. He also found many clay tablets written in the Hittite language. Of course, it took many years before anyone could figure out how to read it. But eventually they did. One interesting thing about Hittite writing was that sometimes the Hittites wrote from right to left on one line and then from left to right on the next.

Further proof that the Hittites had existed was found on clay tablets in Egypt. These clay tablets told of a great battle between Ramses II of Egypt and the Hittites in 1287 B.C. Ramses was even captured by them for a while. He was later rescued when the Egyptians finally won. Archaeologists have even discovered pictures of Hittites drawn by Egyptian artists.

These archaeological discoveries showed that the Bible was correct and that the doubters were completely wrong.

General view of the ruins of the Hittite capital, Hattusa, located about 100 miles east of Ankara in Turkey.

THE WRITING IS STILL ON THE WALL

One of the most interesting stories in the Bible is the one in Daniel chapter 5. It tells about Belshazzar, the last king of Babylon. Belshazzar threw a giant party for a thousand guests. He served them their drinks in cups stolen from God's Temple in Jerusalem.

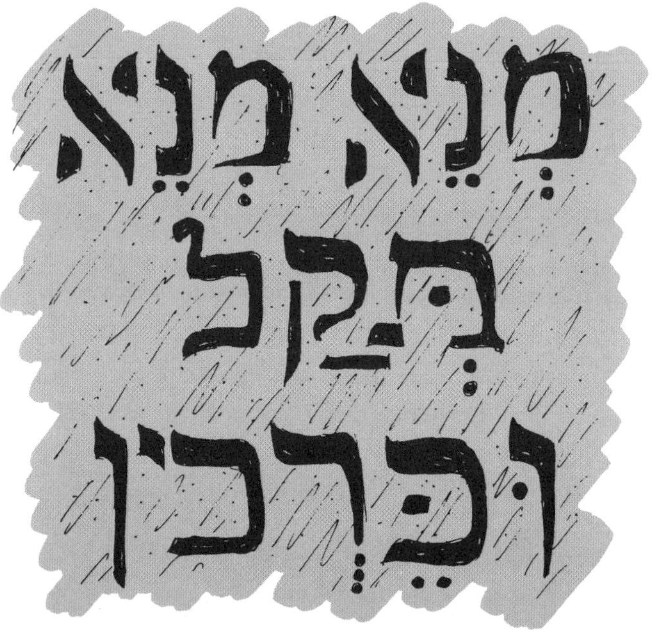

מנא מנא
תקל
ופרסין

Suddenly, a hand appeared, wrote four words on the wall, and then disappeared. The frightened king tried to find out what the words meant. Finally Daniel was called in. Because God revealed to Daniel the meaning of each word, he was able to interpret those words for the king. You can read about the meanings of those words in Daniel 5:26, but what they meant to Belshazzar was that

Sixth-century Babylonian tablet describing a number of historical events, including the taking of Jerusalem.

Belshazzar's time as king was over. He was killed that night, and the Medes and Persians took over Babylon.

For many years, unbelievers said that the story couldn't be true, because Belshazzar was *not* the last king of Babylon. According to the ancient historical writings, Nabonidus was the last king—and there never was a king named Belshazzar.

But in this century, archaeologists digging in the old city of Ur found many tablets that the Babylonians had written on. Some of them were from the time of Nabonidus. And guess what they said? King Nabonidus left the country for several years. While he was gone, he left his son to rule as king. That son was named Belshazzar. He was killed the day the Medes and Persians took over Babylon.

And that, of course, was exactly what the book of Daniel had said.

In school, William Ramsay was an excellent student. Growing up in Scotland, he won several awards for his good grades. And he was especially interested in things that happened long ago. He wanted to learn things about the past that no one else had ever discovered. He made up his mind to learn about the ancient Greeks by actually going to the ruins of their cities. He didn't want to just read about it—he wanted to dig and search until he became an expert on what life was like 2,000 years ago.

But William Ramsay didn't believe the Bible. For example, he didn't believe that the book of Acts in the New Testament was written by Luke, as many Christians believe. He said it was written one hundred years after the time of Luke by someone who didn't know what he was writing about. Ramsay thought the writer just made up some of the stories because they would sound good.

In 1880, Ramsay went on his first expedition to the places described in the book of Acts. He spent many years traveling, digging, and studying ancient writings in that part of the world. He was sure he could prove that the book of Acts was full of mistakes and could not be believed.

And what did he discover? For one thing, he was the first to find out that the city of Iconium was not part of the district of Lycaonia, as the experts in his day used to think. He also found that the people of Lycaonia even spoke their own language. But the book of Acts, which Ramsay didn't believe, had already explained that fact, in chapter 14, verses 1-11.

This Greek inscription on a Roman arch in Thessalonica helped convince Ramsay that the book of Acts was accurate.

Ramsay had not expected his discoveries to prove that the book of Acts was right. But, in fact, the more he discovered, the more he found that Acts was not full of mistakes, after all. He was most impressed with how the writer got those small, seemingly unimportant details exactly right. That, he claimed, was the mark of a writer who knows what he is talking about and is careful to tell everything correctly.

William Ramsay went on to become one of the world's greatest experts on life in New Testament days. His research led him to write many excellent books that show how accurate and believable the New Testament is. In one of those books, he announced that he had become a Christian.

The story of William Ramsay is one more reason we can have confidence that the Bible is true.

nother biblical story that unbelievers used to doubt is found in Genesis 14. There, four kings come all the way from Babylonia to fight five kings in Abraham's area near the Dead Sea. Abraham's nephew, Lot, was captured by the four invaders. Abraham then got a small army together and rescued Lot.

"That couldn't have happened," the doubters said. "It was all made up. The Babylonians didn't have any dealings with the people in Palestine in those days. And anyway, people didn't travel that far back then—especially not to fight."

But in the past hundred years, archaeologists have dug up much information about Babylonia in Abraham's time. It turns out that Babylonia did have dealings with Palestine. They even controlled part of it. And the people from Abraham's area fought to get out from under Babylonian rule more than once. The story in Genesis 14 is obviously one of those times.

Another story that doubters used to criticize is found in Genesis 40—part of the story of Joseph in Egypt. Some people argued that the part about the butler picking grapes to make wine for the king of Egypt wasn't true because there is no evidence that grapes ever grew in Egypt.

But eventually, that evidence was found. In the Egyptian city of Thebes, a painting on a tomb shows Egyptians picking grapes and making wine.

In ancient times, people often carved their writing on stones or clay tablets. This is lucky for us, because those tablets can last for thousands of years. Kings, especially, liked to order tablets carved that would tell of their accomplishments. It is always interesting when these carvings tell of people or events that are also mentioned in the Bible.

For example, Shalmaneser III (king of Assyria from 859-824 B.C.) tells about his dealings with two kings of Israel, Ahab and Jehu. He even has a drawing of Jehu.

Another king of Assyria, Sennacherib, tells the story of his attack on Jerusalem when Hezekiah was king there. That story is also told in the Bible (2 Kings 18:13-19:37).

Right: The Taylor Prism, a hexagonal cylinder, recounts Senacharib's raid into Judah, about 701 B.C.
Above: The "Black Obelisk of Shalmaneser" shows Jehu bowing before Shalmaneser III.

But Sennacherib leaves
out one important part:
why his army wasn't able
to capture Jerusalem.
That isn't surprising, since
those kings didn't usually
tell about their losses,
only their victories.

That's another way the Bible is different from other
ancient books. It tells everything that needs to be
told—victories and defeats, the good and the bad.

The value of these and many other discoveries is
that they help to show over and over again that the
people, places, and events described in the Bible were
real people, places, and events.

More Good Reasons

In many ways, the Bible is the most amazing book ever written. It's really a collection of books. The earliest was written about 1,500 years before Christ. The last book (Revelation) was finished almost 100 years after Jesus' birth. That means it took about 1,600 years to complete the Bible.

Papyrus fragments of John 18:31-33, the earliest copy of any New Testament book, dated about A.D. 150. Found in Egypt.

At least forty different people did part of the writing. And they were all very different! There was Luke (a doctor), Peter (a fisherman), Joshua (an army leader), Amos (a sheep herder), Matthew (a tax collector), Solomon (a king), Nehemiah (a king's servant), and many others we know nothing about.

They wrote from many different places. Moses was traveling in the wilderness. Paul was in prison during part of the time he wrote. Daniel lived in a palace. John was on a lonely island. David was fighting enemies or being chased by them when writing some of the Psalms.

The Bible was first written in three languages. The New Testament was in Greek. Most of the Old Testament was written in Hebrew, but part of Daniel was in Aramaic. The Bible is also made up of many kinds of writings. Part of it is the history of a group of people. Some books follow one person's life. Part of it is poetry; some of the books are collections of laws. There are letters to people and books that tell the future.

Yet this book, written by so many people, over such a long period of time, in different languages, and different places, still all fits together to tell one story of how we got here and where we're going. Things that began in the first book are finished in the last one. Genesis (2:9) tells where God first put the tree of life. Revelation (22:1-3) tells where it is now. Genesis tells the cause of the first sadness. Revelation tells when tears will end.

No man would ever have been able to put together a collection like this!

INDESTRUCTIBLE!

For thousands of years, unbelievers have tried to destroy the Bible, but they have all failed.

This began while the Bible was still being written. In ancient Israel, an evil king, Jehoiakim, burned the book of Jeremiah because it told what he had done wrong. But God helped Jeremiah to write it all again—plus even more (Jeremiah 36).

The Romans and the leaders of the Jews tried to stop Paul by putting him in prison. The prison he was in disappeared long ago. But the letters he wrote while he was there are still helping people today.

In the year 303, the Roman emperor, Diocletian, ordered all copies of the books of the Bible destroyed. He thought that he had succeeded. He even had a medal engraved that said, "The Christian religion is destroyed." But it was Diocletian who died, not the Bible.

Voltaire was a Frenchman who lived in the 1700s. He was a famous writer, but he didn't believe the Scriptures. In fact, he made fun of the Bible. Voltaire predicted that within a hundred years, the Bible would be gone. But fifty years after his death, the printing press he had owned was being used to print Bibles. And the house he had lived in was made into a center for distributing them.

No matter how hard evil men have tried to get rid of the Bible, they haven't been able to. And today, those men are dead. But the Bible remains.

POWER TO CHANGE

here has never been a book
like the Bible. More books have
been written about it than any
other. The message in the Bible
has given artists and musicians
their ideas for many of the
world's greatest masterpieces.

But most important of all, the Scriptures continue to change people's lives. No one can count
the number of people who have turned from a life
of crime, or quit mistreating others, or stopped
using drugs or alcohol after being touched by the
Bible's story.

One of those people was
John Newton, who lived in
the late 1700s. John did
many evil things—in fact, he
spent about ten years buying
and selling people as slaves.
But during one frightening
storm on the high seas, his
ship nearly sank, and
afterward John started
reading the Bible.

It changed his life. Reading Jesus' story in Luke 15
about the runaway son, John realized that God loves
even those of us who have done much wrong, and
he is eager for us to turn to him.

John Newton became a well-known preacher who worked to end the slave business in England. He also wrote several hymns we still sing today—including "Amazing Grace."

Charles Colson had an important White House job working for President Nixon. But he broke the law and was sent to prison. There, he began reading the Bible and turned his life over to Jesus Christ. Now, besides writing best-selling books, he goes to prisons all over the country, telling people about Christ.

Here's another example: Billy Sunday was an alcoholic pro baseball player who was saved and became one of the most famous preachers of his day. Or another: C. S. Lewis was an atheist as a young man but became a believer and went on to author many Christian classics, including the *Narnian Chronicles.*

Many books are interesting and helpful to read. But only the Bible tells us everything we need to know about the things that are most important. As 2 Peter 1:3 says, "Jesus has the power of God. His power has given us everything we need to live and to serve God."

Throughout this book, I have tried to tell some of the many reasons we believe the Bible. Each of these reasons is one more bit of evidence that the Bible came from God.

But what does the Bible itself say? Over and over again, the writers wrote things like this: "This is what the Lord says . . . " (Jeremiah 31:2, NIV) or "The Lord spoke his word to me . . . " (Ezekiel 24:1, ICB).

The Bible tells us that God used the Holy Spirit to tell men what to write. Paul said, "God has shown us these things through the Spirit" (1 Corinthians 2:10, ICB). He said the same thing about the Old Testament: "The Holy Spirit spoke the truth to your fathers through Isaiah the prophet" (Acts 28:25, ICB).

The word we use to say the Bible came from God is "inspiration" or "inspired." That means that God let the writers know what they should write. We don't know exactly how this took place, but Paul wrote in 2 Timothy 3:16 (NIV), "All Scripture is God-breathed." Isn't that an interesting way to describe it? However God gave his message to the writers, it was like he was breathing on them. To help us understand better, Peter adds this explanation:

> Most of all you must understand this: No prophecy in the Scriptures ever comes from the prophet's own interpretation. No prophecy ever came from what a man wanted to say. But men led by the Holy Spirit spoke words from God.
>
> (2 Peter 1:20–21, ICB)

The Bible writers wanted to be sure that we understood that they were not just giving their own ideas. Rather, God himself was giving them information to pass on to us.

Because of that, we can be sure that the Bible is God's message to us. As we read it carefully, let's remember 2 Timothy 3:15 (ICB): "The Scriptures are able to make you wise. And that wisdom leads to salvation through faith in Christ Jesus."

MORE GOOD BOOKS TO READ!

You may want to read more about the things discussed in this book. Here are a few good places to start.

Kenny Barfield. *Why the Bible is Number One.* Grand Rapids, Michigan: Baker Book House, 1988.

Batsell Baxter. *I Believe Because.* Grand Rapids: Baker Book House, 1971.

F. F. Bruce. *The New Testament Documents—Are They Reliable?* Grand Rapids: Eerdmans Publishing, 1959.

D. James Kennedy. *Why I Believe.* Dallas, Texas: Word Publishing, 1981.

Josh McDowell. *Evidence That Demands a Verdict.* San Bernardino: Here's Life Publishers, 1979.

S. I. McMillen. *None of These Diseases.* Old Tappan, New Jersey: Fleming H. Revell, 1984.

William Ramsay. *St. Paul the Traveller and Roman Citizen.* Grand Rapids: Baker Book House, 1982.

Lawrence Richards. *It Couldn't Just Happen.* Dallas: Word Publishing, 1987.

J. A. Thompson. *The Bible and Archaeology.* Grand Rapids: Eerdmans Publishing, 1972.